PAIN DIARY:

Working Methadone

&

The Life &Times of the Man Sawed in Half

PAIN DIARY:
Working Methadone
&
The Life & Times of the Man Sawed in Half

Poems by Joseph D. Reich

Cover Art: © Christopher Howey | Dreamstime.com

Library of Congress Control Number: 2010935509
ISBN-13: 978-0-9841005-3-8
ISBN-10: 0-9841005-3-9

Published by Brick Road Poetry Press
P. O. Box 751
Columbus, GA 31902-0751
www.brickroadpoetrypress.com
Brick Road logo by Dwight New

CONTENTS

Working Methadone   1-59

The Life & Times of the Man Sawed in Half   61-95

Part I:

Working Methadone

For The Fishermen

"I spoke into his eyes, I thought you died alone"

-Bowie

1. *Call Me Ishmael, I Mean... "Call Me, Ishmael!"*

                  *

you arrive in the dark
            at dawn to the docks

                        ...to silhouettes

                              smoking cigarettes
                                    waving at me from afar

                  *

nod at the security guard

                  *

it appears there are some really kind & classy
                  on the go, workaholic melancholics here

            hope i can keep up with them...
                        hope they keep me here

                  *

exchanging words & worries
            stories & pleasantries

                        with all the pretty portuguese secretaries

            sentimentally reflecting back to my days in spain
                        barcelona, sevilla, cordoba

*

on my lunch break i sit in my car
          listening to sports radio

*

a bluebird rests
        contemplative on cattail

*

i mosey on over to moby dick river
       & imbibe all the elements

             of a wild, untamed ocean

   & imagine how melville one fine dawn
               simply shoved off from shore

                  for some action & adventure

        sleeping with one eye open
              transformed, reborn.

*

in a little room down a long hall
       j/eases looks into the filthy, cracked mirror

           haunted, disassociated
       keen, unfamiliar

    intuitive

down in the dumps
on the run

knowing it all
in deep, nihilistic spirit

...transcendent

*

he is no different
than any one of these dope addicts

*

& if in fact you call this a habit
"a drug habit"

then i have so much more tolerance
than any of the pettiness of any of

the pricks i have experienced
in this thing called "existence"

if you get my drift

she has a habit to...
he has a habit of...

their culture has...
cultivated...

*

somewhere between suicidal & homicidal
                    is this false game of survival

                                    called "denial"

                *

"hey, it was such a nice day today
                i decided to put together my motorcycle!"

            "they were giving away tickets over my radio station"

                *

clattering hoofbeats beat past my door
        of some tragic, angelic social worker out to save the world

                    or at least a couple of lost souls
                            for their dose of methadone

                *

when she gets home
        she will take off all her clothes

    her mask & thighs & eyes
                her high heels
                    & blouse & brassiere

                            drop her panties
                                & let it all go

let it all flow
in a flood of tears

you wonder what's for supper?

*

it's funny because i am supposed to be
this real supportive, compassionate social worker

here to save lives & often do & often can't change mine
& help to refrain & reframe

to maintain & not to die & thrive

where just outside my door is all the folklore
of that deep blue sea & me locked inside

& ironically feel like one of his most intriguing, impossible
characters just a century later–

"i prefer not to...
i prefer not to"

*

junkie shuffles down the hall
& all you hear is–

"and i think..."

...therefore i am?

*

what's random is splendid
                    ...unexpected

                        & you want to be remembered
                                    as some kind of ghost

            some sort of phantom
                        that kept them all laughing

            *

while in the deep dark night
            of morning
                just off the highway

                        you see
                            set back on a billboard

                                paul revere's horse
                                    neon knock-knees
                                            clapping

            *

not too far off
            from moby dick marina

                    across the river
                            from the methadone clinic

*

   & think–

wow...

this is all we got

left to show for it?

2. *Rough Days, You Feel Alive*

t'night pon drinkin coal red wine on ice
i fell like jesus christ with all da tings
bin gone thru reachin jus gett'n fiyed
offer all i did for these bastids &
whore work & sacrifices now contessing
my unploymen & scotts lawn threaten'n
my wife over da telephone gong to collections
& thaw maybe with hard clothes & soul
on hole i not him & juss apre she hate
the buzz when you kin in thee why whip
pen win & decide in stead to sim plea look at chris
miss lites across the block & watch local cable station
an ounce sing *leaf pick up bridge open'n* & *8th grade girls quire*
siren night hollee nigh how at the methdone clinic i work in i feel
so much simptea exactly like them for simply making one wrong
turn (sun them cheerleaders stray a stew dens fish'men) how jus
miss brook land & harlen so much taken k-arm-a trains home
lone at dawn to my ten men in forest to the ocean to my bones

3. *Low Man On Totem Pole*

they finally gave me my office
and it looks straight across
to fish houses

to dock workers steering
fish to the horizon
that breaks

like eggs over
easy easing
over toast

in
the
morning

dragging dollies
of crustaceans their
skull-ups & *soarfish*

the squawk of savage seagulls
come in for their landing and take
their place way atop telephone poles

seaport birds flapping to tops of filthy poles
like all those radiant ancient seaports from
so long ago from around the world

taking to lugubrious lamplight
to lugubrious sky to lugubrious life
ships come in from night right on time

4. *The Netherworld*

when you suddenly see
like some surreal spiritual dream
spitting spools of scarlet sunlight

splashed out against
whitewashed walls
of the fish factory

as if in some
dreary radiant drive-
in awe and antiquity

5. *Working Methadone*

both me and the good
ol' fishermen trying to get clean
mutually agree while loosely laughing–

"who are our
super heroes?"

that seemed
to sum up
everything

6. *Afternoons*

on these gray days i love to see
their silky white wings swooping
and sailing past my window with
their wild woeful whistling visiting
my lonesome being and wonder
when it was when god invented
them the exact time and date
and place that they came into
being welcoming all strangers
& women & men & children
from other races & realities
reverberating echoing
throughout the beautiful
tragedy of timeless history

7. *Fog Of The Ages*

as their long lonesome
call calls me back
to lovely holy
boxcar diners
set back dug
deep into the
weeds of jersey
junkies dreaming
like jack-o-lanterns in lobby
dazed and dreary some of them
even precious and pretty and can't
help but to feel a certain amount of
affinity or even a strange and subtle
affection of magical mystery
like ravishing girls from sicily
when you wait at dawn at some
wind-swept café for the ferry
reflective and redeemed brain
dead and brooding dead dogs
passed out beneath palm trees
sighing solemnly and a sea
sounding little something like
...so it seems, so it seems
so it seems, so it seems

8. *The Origins Of Slapstick Comedy*

some of them just sit there
slumped over in chairs
like these sad slapstick
laurel & hardy characters

moping with mops of rag doll hair
like those raggedy anns that used to
just collapse in the corner of bedrooms

with their wild and wicked stares
silent and introspective brooding
and blue full of down in the dump
gloom and doom old white paint

on worn-out work shoes patiently waiting
to be dosed at dawn with stars still strung up
strung out in the sky in lovely lamp moonlight

9. *Black & Blue*

driving through the deep
dark dawn you imagine

signs on the side of
the road which read
"attractions/sea"

the weather on
the radio which
predicts "windy"

and junkies
being delivered
in yellow taxis
to their destiny

10. *Punchline*

really nice hard working construction guys
ramble through the early dark morning of light
to pick up their daily dose to try and start a new life

11. *Weather*

a faded gold sign
stuck to red brick
which reads—

river coat
company

12. *Close To Rock Bottom*

*

i close my eyes in the fluorescent light of my opaquely-lit office
and begin to fantasize and think back to all those wild women
i once knew in my past life all those sweet secret orifices entered

fine-woven spectacular spectrums of blonde & brunette & scarlet
those moments relationships memories experiences
with eyes shut tight thinking back to those times
could anything have been much better?

*

i look up at the recovery group lists which read...
"alice's recovery, katie's recovery, heather's
recovery skills" and know as well as you do
that these kind and confused cherubs really
of gloom and doom from social work schools
will even come as far out as the state of california
desperate and innocent for some holy misbegotten
reason just to hook up and eat up some hopeless
helpless schmuck in the hopes just to spend a little time
in tiny flats out in new bedford during the holiday season

*

they laugh and smile
trying to make it
all worthwhile

*

Intermission:

and every so often i'll look up at the computer screen
at dose history (*dozing history*), ua's, episodes
and all these brilliant and beautiful girls
sometimes 20-21 years old and wonder

where it all went wrong resembling
some stunning frida kahlo from
the portuguese slums
of pitiful shores

*

these victims these martyrs
just trying to keep their heads
above water by any means possible

*

and you got to be like this charlie chan
character having to re-piece together
the parts of the puzzle
and place it back
on the wall

*

you hear two men in the hall
pass past your door–

"how you doing, alright?"
"just hanging on by a thread"
"i hear you..."

*

"attention please, attention please...
the copier will be down for about a half-hour
i'll let you know when you can start printing up notes"

*

you shut your eyes again and start naturally singing–
"princess so alarming though my love is never charming
life is just a cocktail party on the street..."

*

sometimes i even find *myself* having cravings
more specifically from back in the day

for american cheese & butter & wonder bread sandwiches
slouching on summer porches contemplative & contented

*

for hot pretzels from manhattan outside
madison square garden on days more like
mad nights of the good ol' knickerbockers
which starred earl "the pearl" monroe with

his famous fade-away jumper, walt "clyde" frazier
in pimp hat and fur coat and swagger, bill bradley
the rhodes scholar, dave debusschere and a
"nice garden welcome for hawww-thawn winnn-go!"

*

crowding courtside during warm-ups all dressed
up as a cute curious child with my hard working
father scaling the towering torso of willis reed
in awe and inquisitively inquiring with gusto–

"is he bigger than god?"

similar to being in a dark movie theater
with my mom watching "the sting"
for the first time ever and asking–
"where are their wives?"

*

getting back to that portuguese secretary packed
perfectly into tight black jeans with her smooth olive
skin and olive eyes as deep as the sea she comes from
the azores lisbon imagining her in the chart room opening
and closing the wall with that big safe-like wheel just right
so you might make it a tight squeeze and her not moving
deliberately even protruding and placing that pretty peace

*

End Of Intermission:

all these eager angels look and sound exactly like
those soulful school teachers from your childhood
when you never even knew how miserable and blue

*

mrs. cardasis with her fresh ripe thighs
spread apart on her fold-out chair reading
children's books and us seated there without
a care strewn out on the floor truth or dare kids
only to find out i swear she was wearing no underwear

*

seduced stunned and scared
like some eternal game
of freeze tag

*

knowing right there and then
somehow somewhere

that these women
these wild girls

you never had
a fighting chance

*

"red rover, red rover
let joey come over"

and you take a deep breath
and start to inch forward...

13. *Internal Referral*

"Reason For Increase"	"Decrease"
gooseflesh	lethargy
restlessness	sleepy
craving to use opiates	slurred
chills and flashes	speech

14. *Demographic: Mug Shot*

whenever you look at the face
sheet they always seem to have
that strange and sad look on their
face like how did i get myself to this
godforsaken place eternally stunned
bummed displaced and out of place

15. *Things I Used To Like To Think Of From Childhood*

a) the rags to riches story of the beatles

b) bounding barefoot bare-chested
    to that lit vending machine
    on the balcony

c) of a brilliant warm caribbean evening

d) maybe even antigua

e) *raid on entebbe*

f) its simple buzz held more meaning...

16. *Often When I See*

all these dramas unfold in relationships
in the workplace families and cultures
i just want to fold them back up and
toss them right back in the garbage

(not necessarily convinced
that when man gets older he gets
more distinguished or compassionate
yet more so something of a sociopath

think of the plight
of old man goirot
raskolnikov romeo
how they got crossed)

and be like what do you
call that? a fire-setter?

17. *Basquiat*

a white sign
outside the dump
with faded black letters

tells us the date and
times for leaf drop off

18. *Ideations*

black crows
sit way a top
drizzly trees

and find myself just beginning to relate
to all those who try to do the deed either by
hanging putting a bullet in the brain or o.d.'ing

without all of that
silly letter writing

or friends and family
reuniting all for the sake
of hearing their own vain voices
chiming in with corny chattering

19. *When Nietzsche Said "God Is Dead"*

i think what he really meant
was that in an environment
where all that simply exists are
white devils with so little culture

flavor integrity honor and rhythm sense
of humor soul brother soul sister welcome to the
suburbs how much you feel the absence of a savior

scholars like to say he was prophetic...
really what he was was a social observer

20. *Channel X*

ours is a culture of complaining look how the athlete
interacts with the referee caught up in a useless cycle
of blaming never taking any responsibility these reality

show kids with their cellphone attitudes in malls in auto-
mobiles in schools political and social forum horrible
cities and suburbs cruel corporations gun-ho ghettos

lower the dosage increase the dosage yet forget the cause
not been a cause for so damn long drive-thru bullethole
soulless soul everything-must-go gathered around the talk
show glamorized herd about as mediocre as they come

i have always trusted more
those with the schizophrenia

with the obsessive-
compulsive
disorder

("i knew i was in trouble 'cause i passed out and heard trains
in my ears but there were no trains anywhere..." he giggles
modest and humble kindest person you'd ever want to know)

the goal-oriented
go-getter always
left so much
to be desired

21. *Loner*

o how i envied emily dickinson and marcel proust
locked up in lovely little lavish roosts
writing till their hearts' content

out in montmartre
and massachusetts looking out
over the witches & wildernesses

every so often the pizza man
& wine man & ice man
dropping off their loot

their maids
& mistresses
& piano tuner

or sometimes might retreat
to the woods & kingdom to get
their helping of the latest news & gossip

stealing firewood, glances
at dances, hearts & souls
diagnoses...

and can only imagine them
in their bathrobe and victorian dress
neurotic, nihilistic, with a bit of self-neglect

yet so keenly in touch with the
hypocrisies & contradictions
of the human condition

clinging & celebrating
the capricious change of seasons
(the last days of socrates & nietzsche)

silhouettes pressed against the lattice
and how people must have made fun of them
ignorant & oblivious that they were writing words

that would forever transcend generations...
i suppose that this is the fate, the faith of every great
artist; to be looked at as something of a freak or grotesque

kaf-
ka-
esque

and still willing to sacrifice
their scones, their bones
for the greater good

of what we deem
to be "culture
& civilization"

the methadone clinic sits in beet red brick
of blustery blue firmament across the river from the moby
dick marina with homes composed of crows & bulletholes

suppose you just gotta roll
and know the grander
scheme of things

i've always been
something of
a thief

22. *Something*

like edgar allen poe
shooting up dope
later on turning
to ginsberg
searching
for similar
way to cope
in the same
rainy run-
down lower-
east side
cobble
stone

23. *A Lot Like The Plot Of Madame Plath*

"don't you think hell
would be if you were forced to have
to live the exact same life backwards?"

24. *Frank's Plight*

brother shrieking at sister
beneath rainy movie theater–
"i'm not proud i'm a junkie!"

25. *Over The River And I'll See You In The Funnies*

later on we found out he held up
a jewelry store as it was on the 10
o'clock news and swore–"o shit...isn't?"

26. *Soothsayer's Sons*

strangely enough
these were always the neighbors you
felt you could trust and felt most comfortable

27. *Where Foghorns Hail From*

heading home with your cheeseburger
and chocolate shake from the diner
beneath midnight cherry blossom

28. *Alley-View*

to a room
chock full
of technicolor

edward g.
robinson
on the run

29. *Art Of Landscaping*

word around the cul-de-sac to be kept on the hush-hush
was that she finally asked him for a divorce her drinking
cheating husband and even more so found ourselves
shocked that she had not asked for one much earlier

funny that dark home
with the electricity
always on

watch out
here comes
the rain and wind

the
crimes
of man...

30. *Vantage Point*

you sit in the peaceful puddly
parking lot of deep dark dusk
waiting for chinese take-out

at the miniature golf course
right around the corner from
some all-gentleman's club

decked out in powder-pink
"rated #1 in all of..." right in front
of a very exclusive privately-gated

community of lego-like
condominiums in which
you need a key in order

to
fit
in

waiting for your crab rangoon
and steamed dumplings with
a sign looking down on you

go coast guard...

31. *The Package*

yesterday when i got home from work
there was a package in our driveway

addressed to dylan jacob reich
from phillip and phyllis schmutz

a package was in our driveway
from phillip and phyllis schmutz

there was a package for dylan jacob
from phillip and phyllis schmutz...

32. *Somewhere 'Round Sundown*

fox yawns
and slips
back to the
wilderness

33. *Bones 'N A Bag Of Wind*

i think i heard my wife say the other day—
"the boat, the ghost, goes to nantucket
and martha's vineyard" boats and ghosts,

a boat full of ghost, air-conditioned citizen,
charter, carnival, clown's mouth, cathedral,
sweltering winds of suburban train stations

full of repressed, rigid citizens with no soul no vision,
this appears to be their lifestyle and language, their jus-
tification... existence; the closer you get to caucasians the
more you feel their contradictions (loss and abandonment)
yet they all play the role of good family men, hard-working
husbands, as you see their expressions switch in a second

what a disappointment! is this what you might conveniently
call culture & civilization in america? a call on your cellular?
fragmentation? alienation? competition? religion? like some
pompous punchline at the end of a pathetic procession?
the speeches & food no different at the country club
or funeral... as the train crawling into grand central

while you miss most of all the lampposts and pumpkins
lower east side functions (all the upper east side girls
voyeuristic and defensive) the puerto rican girls hanging
from hot sills of south brooklyn casket; you miss too the
brilliant outskirts which is really the radiant core of civilization

...the irish sea, bay of naples, hudson river, barbers and robbers
of barcelona, old men from naples hysterically pretending to
flog each other with opened-up fold-out chairs on the corner;
black girl who's blind father used to own a string of bodegas and
would mail you profound postcards that would happen to mention–

"there are real bums out here in san francisco"
and you knew exactly what she was referring to
and this you could sincerely relate to far more than
any wedding-bar-mitzvah-invitation meant to represent
some pleasant & pathetic life-transition... you hear your girl

babbling to your son something that sounds a lot like blues
and bible in the kitchen, crazy gymnasiums, brawls at the dean
of discipline, all the virgins have turned to exhibitionism in
the depressed towns of new england, heroin, black men...

34. *Days Of Detention*

i remember my idiot professor from way back in the day
who told us he thought holden caulfield had gone crazy for
punching out all the windows of his garage door and how
i even recall i thought *he* was crazy for not understanding

35. *As For Me*

i'd rather
throw a toast
to the ghosts

36. *Rogue Scholar*

before i go i'm not gonna
go to holy mecca but to reunite
with all those friends i lost a long
time ago in detroit more specifically
in dearborn and the arab community

polson montana to the deep bleak
indian reservation to try and find my
fugitive friend always on the run and
imbibe in one final punchline to st. louis
and my old pal who turned to alcohol and
found gunned down in the alley and good ol' oklahoma
to have one last shot with soulmate from new york city

37. *Spitting Image*

i swear all my "patients" these days want to escape
to the sunshine state or get a transfer out of this place
(asking "can you get me a transfer?" like i'm some kind
of travel agent) to las vegas to get into trouble or back to

the hustle or black market to literally break the bank yet in
actuality i can't fault them for back in the day i was just as guilty

38. *Manifest Destiny*

they made
& created
& constructed
these states
they celebrated
& commiserated
& staked out
these states
born & raised
off orchards
& plantain
& burritos
& mad dog 20/20
hamburger helper
& sloppy joes &
shake & bake
& american
chow mein
& so we go
to seek out
these states
to escape
to find a way...
can't tell you how many times
i went back & forth between
n.y. & l.a. & reno & seattle
& portland & san francisco
all those criminals i came across
some of the kindest strangers
some of the keenest creatures
you'd ever want to know
the radiant girls
& wild child
having traveled

miles & miles
just to find
just to reveal
just to feel good
about themselves
& the almost impossible
phantasmagorical stories that
were told bright-eyed & bold
quasimodo having crept
deep from within dingy
dungeon of a shattered
soul out of plato's cave
up the fire escape
to the belfry
to the stars
to now expose
a brand-new
wardrobe of
the king's clothes
a cast of characters
having been cast away
literally having runaway
from institutions
reform schools
private schools ghettos
splendor screen doors
steeples and the law
to figure out a way of
somehow getting on
and so we search
for these states
to escape
a state of
diss/grace
of shame
of guilt
& games
of how they
make you feel
about yourself
no longer afraid

cold & crazed
a sacred
mistaken
identity
regenerated
to rid ourselves
to redeem ourselves
of brainwash & blame
of the state we're in
and realize a whole
other different state
so many of us violated
and raped displaced!
displaced! displaced!
alas to discover
diss-place!
feeling your soul
literally begin
to leap
& stir
& race
when you see
the glimmering gates
& bridges & towers
of san francisco
rise up from
the secret
unbelievable
pageantry
of the pacific
starving
intuitive
blessed!
and it all makes
perfect sense
in one single
solitary soulful
spontaneous
moment
of which
they cannot

& will never
steal from you
made these states...

39. *Duel Diagnoses: Suicidal/Homicidal*

in the storage room
they got boxes upon
boxes upon boxes of

tissues

if only you knew
everything they've been through
a matter of fact it would be a pure

understatement
to call any of
these issues

40. *Shout-Out*

the exhibits in the midnight muse/am
take a deep breath and soulfully sigh
pharaohs from ancient egypt
greek gods and african tribes

while silently staring out
brooding bleak windows
into the transcendent radiant night
as all i can say is god bless my wife

41. *Cold Front: Prodromal Stage*

it felt at certain points
of life like sometimes
you almost had to beg
friends to be nice and
might even take it on

yourself like you had done
something wrong when you
were still the exact same
imaginative and kind soul
with a zest and gusto for life

as they were starting to develop
those cruel and contradictory
characterological traits
of which grown ups

become so famous for
of jealousy and envy leaving you
constantly to be worrying and wondering
beating yourself up like did i do something

you'd spend hours days
reflecting tracing reflections
of tall pine trees swaying freely
in the faded mirror of your mother's

dressing room table contemplating
and considering having a subtle
and soothing-like feeling

god if i could take back
those feelings
those days
of losers

making me feel
so lost and lonely
little and lousy...

42. *See*

i think my p.t.s.d.
caught p.t.s.d.
and finally

at last
i am free

43. *Mommy*

in many ways daddy saw me simply as an extension to himself
and so strangely and perversely he ended up looking up to me
and when i turned out to be what he had not hoped me to be

ended up turning angry
not only rejecting me
yet in many ways

himself...
his core identity
being and reality

there's really not
much more i can say
i really had nothing...

44. *Notes From The East*

taking me practically a lifetime to find my-
self yet when i stop to think about it
i'd really like to get lost again

things just seemed so much more interesting then
capturing keen visions of my reincarnation
beautiful tomboys from new england

waiting
on their
methadone

45. *Mid-Life*

so is it so wrong for me
to imagine all our babysitters
disrobed in a glow around the dining
room table dropping silverware and
me being grateful and feeding them a feast
high on wine tipsy loopy giddy for the tee-hee-
hee girls whispering laughing blushing having
a hell of a good time and me spooning them punch-
lines i mean isn't that really the only way to get by?

46. *Riding Bikes Back From School*

tonight upon spooning
with my wife
she said

something like–
"you know with polenta
the skies are the limit..."

and
thought
to myself

could any-
one really ar-
gue with this?

47. *How A Swamp Comes To Life*

the sound of my baby boy's
lullabies break my heart
like the raindrops
on the roof
of the asylum
drive-in
burnt-out
dance hall
and boardwalk
movie theater
after coming out
of staticky nostalgia
from years and years of
classic drama wondering if
there's any mail in the mailbox
pondering who's playing for the "live
entertainment" at the chinese liquid lounge
knowing for sure the human cannonball
fire swallower dog-faced boy are all just
trying to figure out their way back home

48. *Opinion's Like An Asshole: Everyone's Got One*

back in the day they used to say such things
like it was so safe and what a low crime rate
to live in certain places like little italy as no

one would ever even dare to think to try a thing
due to the influence of john gotti as i was never
quite sure or convinced how much i necessarily
agreed with this type of sweeping and simplistic
reasoning while i used to reside in the lower east side

12th street more exactly where lucky luciano
used to hatch up his sicilian schemes and now
resides the jamaican posse of which i became really
quite friendly judah and snowball who used to give me

goats heads and ginger beer and rice and peas and
hawaiian gold for free but not to get on the wrong side
of them or cross them or to become an enemy as they
would instantly turn on you and chop you into a million
pieces brandishing big bold machetes as these days
i wonder who and what and where and if there is any-
thing out there that might protect me while listening to
eminem and dido and miss e. and good ol' bob marley

drifting through the deep dark evening of morning
to the clinic on the sea and all those dead end streets
named after different types of whaling all the lumbermen
and landscapers heading to their destiny all the portuguese
and vietnamese fishermen strung out on d.–"why can't we be
what we want to be/we want to be free..." as simple as these
few key lines of beauty and suddenly find myself sheepishly
laughing triggering me back to all those naive blissful
feelings and times from divine days of dreaming

a sunoco sign sailing, as though magically suspended
sharp & solitary in a blue topaz sky, brilliant
& bright like blazing hot lightning rods

passed down from great
mythological gods

what a wreck some of them are
these towns these stars–

"hey mr. cop, ain't go no..."
"hey!"
"hey!"
"hey mr. cop..."

49. *Bloodshot*

you get so sick of trying to figure out the sick shit
of the sick human mind which often seems like
a cross between the sadistic and the sublime

shakespeare and eugene o'neill and moliere
tried to psychologically and subliminally
sentimentally deconstruct all these crimes

and that is why i often simply find myself
turning to sex and the texture of seasons
which always seems to cut through lies

remember how you felt after all of that time
after you immersed your fragile body beneath the lake
in the mountainside your fragile face beneath the shower

after doing all that jail time
it never quite seemed to matter
all these guys old girlfriends and

clients won't think twice
about turning on you
on a dime

were always able to relate
to clouseau when he subtly
snickered under his breath

under the influence
of stress the infamous
punch line—"filthy swine"

50. *Babylon*

like i would have loved to have
met the prop man from the 3 stooges
around the time of the 20s & 30s & 40s
out in hollywoodland probably
in the state of a late
early california evening
traipsing through
black & white static
in my casually wrinkled

linen wandering to whitewashed
studios as he'd show me everything
the scalpels & saws & tweezers
the hammers & nails & doctors bags
& paint cans & ladders then perhaps reveal
all his secret haunts & hideaways (maybe even
running into a brando or clark gable or cary grant)
he'd be a real swell guy & we'd get
high for a couple of nights off vodka
gimlets & dry martinis & maybe
if i got lucky might even set me
up for a chance meeting with
those mad jewish cousins
from brooklyn that being
of course larry moe & curly
also being a bunch of regular
joes simply looking to make
a nice living off the bleak
tragedy & routines
of everyday living

51. *Delancey*

can someone please tell me
the spelling of that old yiddish
proverb–"hock-a-me-ka-china"

which means exactly what it sounds
like like some slow skittering skiff
that never quite gets around

while your loved one eloquently exclaims–
"you're giving me a hock-a-me-ka-china"
translation:

"you could give
a headache to a
fuckin' aspirin!"

52. *Proof Of Being There*

just discovered note on top of my desk
which simply said "proof of being there"

where this kid had left me a message
that they had finally caught up with him

and wanted me to fax out to his probation
officer he had been here for his 10:30 dosing

upon further reflection
i really don't think...

yet he was a good kid
and would have done anything

to see if i might maybe be able
to provide him "proof of being..."

53. *When I Sit In My Office Slain*

and feel totally drained
i think of that hog farm
from just around the way

pigs and piglets of the hog farm
which dissolve all doubts and
worries and suddenly turn calm

you imagine signs
"thickly settled/cats"
and mailboxes set back

in the leafy autumnal swamps
with long lichen branches
hanging off

after some shakespearean storm
with those torn terrible tragic
chandeliers about to fall

and squirrels who scuttle up
bare branches of apple trees in fall
to the bells & whistles & shattered

light-
bulbs
of heaven

snail shells curiously
embedded in clapboard
with the clitter-clatter

of the distant
windchime
echoes

corn having been stripped off
stalks leaving just the brittle
beautiful bones of scarecrows

54. *Track*

you drift down these long white halls
and suddenly recall those days when
you had to come in out of the rain and

felt a certain amount of comfort and certainty
in racing short gym shorts scattering perfectly
awkward pre-pubescent bodies past the lockers

through dim hallways
with thunder and lightning
going off in wild windowpanes

feeling a bizarre sense of belonging
of strange detached longing never quite feeling
a part of the thundering herd usually used to being

chased by some sadistic napoleonic vice principal
with his hollow and sunken complexion blaring behind bleary-
eyed bifocals threatening multiple detentions and suspensions

as though he was caught in some sort
of sadistic arrested stage of development
and was trying to get back at you for all the times

he had felt betrayed
bullied and
beaten

55. *Little Something Like Beefsteak Charlies*

where all your and you wise ass buddies
passed around blunts outside the hayden
planetarium before you made your way
to the pink floyd light show stoned and
wasted you believe somewhere deep
in the upper east side then staggered
to beefsteak charlies to imbibe in all
the all you can eat as advertised
steak and shrimp and wine but
had to find a way to devein and
strip off the underside and millions
of legs and impossible shells and
get by on watered down sangria
and by the time you were all done
with these terribly detailed and delicate
things that didn't quite seem to measure
up exactly to the liberating commercial seen
on t.v. simply wanted to get the hell out of there
and agree you were happy and return to the evening
back to your safe bedroom to go and hit the sheets

56. *Mail Call*

you contemplate like
d. tracy behind dusty blinds
trying desperately not to lose your mind

the drug counselor with bankers' hours
able to watch the dusk draw to nightfall
and widow screw in her electric candles

often you feel like you're just barely hanging on
like one of those gross glossy calendars
in a fast food chinese take-out

with brilliant corny photos
from the mainland
of hong kong

dangling
off some
dirty wall

what i have to be grateful for is a wife who
everytime around this hour turns our home
into a pagoda of eclectic smells and aromas

57. *Restful Valley*

and know this really is
an unrealistic image but i
would love to see a whole
tribe of indians storm in from
the dakotas or montana into one
of those perfect private manicured
exclusive condominium complex
subdivisions made up of marigolds
and mailboxes suddenly appearing
out of nowhere in their tribal costume
riding bareback with bows and arrows

and for no apparent reason shoot up
the whole neighborhood pulling back
bows and plunging arrows into the backs
of those fat know-it-all caucasians going off
at the mouth cigar dropping out right around
backyard barbeques riding off with their filthy
gossipy wives and pseudo-seductive sheltered
borderline daughters in britney spears colors
the only ones left will be the dogs behind invisible fences
who take cat-naps with their paws pointed up to heaven

58. *Garage Door Revelations*

on some days
on some nights
i like to simply
take shelter in my garage
and watch the draining day
gradually fade into night
with streaks of pink and purple light
at the edge of the wild wilderness
and the silhouettes of long tall
pines start to shake in the sky
and you feel and hear all the
universe stir from deep within
the depths of your garage on
the border of darkness and light
strangely enough this is when
i feel most alive when the swamp
sighs and what i'd like to think
might be a coyote cry and no
nagging wife and children get
out their final wild howls before
they slip in for supper as you've become
that neighbor that no one really knows about
which makes me all that much more satisfied
like some character out of a faulkner or balzac
novel yet really the kindest man alive
on this side of the mississippi

but since we're pretty far
from there i'd like to say
lake erie as the sleek bleak
teeth of evening start to sink
into the bloody meat of brooding
and there's no need any longer for
any type of speaking as everything
begins to lose meaning and acquire
mystery and all that's left is wondering
gushing and glowing radiant and redeemed
and my figure starts to fade with the leftover
mums and hibiscus still lingering in the garage
the sitters will be over soon
to tell us all about their love lives

59. *Days Of Lichen*

what do you think it would be like
a whole house that talks in its sleep?
do you think that would be cool or kind
of creepy with some solitary cat creeping
past the keyholes in the deep dark
evening and wintery silhouetted
scenes maybe even a fox and
coyote and a whole house
going off at the mouth
chattering at three
in the morning

do you think that would
be cool or kind of creepy?
i think it might be some-
where in between kind of
how i feel about humanity

60. *Just Like Joe Buck*

and it has only been until just recently
that i have been having these recurring
dreams not really so recent or recurring
but more so solitary and isolating having
to pick up some weekend guest at the airport
and not really knowing who it is while obscurely
finding this so much more intriguing
the notion of not knowing
having spent the last
10 20 30 years...

doing a lot of self-analysis
and soul-searching realizing
that this stranger is "me" feeling
this mild extreme deep-seated
feeling of eternally feeling an un-
wanted sense of self-loathing and dis-
belief living the self-fulfilling prophecy
yet not really even so much caring
and thus looking more so forward
to picking up this long-lost stranger
without a name or identity perversely
profoundly holding more meaning

my greatest times invariably
having always been in rambling

they tell us we're "not to leave"
the methadone people
the junkies

alone
in our
office

as for example when we go
to the chart room or bathroom
and always found this rule to be
so futile and silly *attention-seeking?*

paradoxically telling
us we are there to
restore their self-
respect and dignity

(and will even go
out of my way to be
in direct and blatant
disregard and violation)

like what are they gonna do?
steal my jung my freud my camus?

and in many ways dream that they do
as when i happen to return back
seeing them all in disarray
and rearranged hoping

that they're gonna be able
to extract as much meaning
from these things as me

these long-lost lonely
strangers of anonymity
taking in the symbols and archetypes
of an uncertain conscious unconscious reality

61. *Cherry Blossom*

after i perform pretty decent counseling
unconditionally supportive and compassionate with a bit
of redirecting and reflecting i finally have good dreams

with those tall towering cherry blossom of white cotton
blooming and budding beneath all that rain and fog
and forests and frogs trauma and damaged role

playing and mythology and sometimes just sometimes
you might experience the keen image of silhouetted
cherry blossom tumbling & towering towards the sky

remember how you always felt
when you saw a deer suddenly leap
out of the forest in the dusk of fog?

how you strangely always knew
like finally having sweet dream
after all that's gone wrong...

62. *Being ~The Etymology Of Dreaming*

i want to know
where does fox go?
(the seagull & crow)
where does coyote sleep
in the deep, dark night?
on a blanket of leaves?
right by the cypress tree?
near a secret stream?
nestled, entwined, nuzzling
side by side on the riverside?
beneath moonlight?
how do they sigh? judge time?
& so maybe he really is not so sly
& just trying to get by like you & i
with the same absurd, desperate need
to cry, nameless, aimless, shy; harmless,
alone, kind & alive, waking up to live the
same old lie, to die, to try & survive, knowing
deep down inside it's always the same eternal
question of why; why you sleep on a cold, hard
floor at the foot of your bed, dead, beneath her toes
where the illusion ends & spirit begins, the final validation,
definition, that at last separates virtue from sin & binds her
to him & you spiritually know where the fox goes, where coyote
glows, so many moons ago, something you've always known, what

they can never ever begin to know, how you will continue to persist
& grow, which is your impenetrable, transcendent, incandescent soul

63. *Days Of Hamlet*

and so you keep on having this dream
where your ship crashes into some sand
reef and you bang your knee and gotta pee
where there's no need to "abandon ship, abandon ship"
cause you been fighting and fleeing for so damn long you no longer
feel any feeling at all or make any true distinction between belief
and non-belief can't even fathom such things and thus
the necessary state of dreaming
where the soup
of the day is
alphabet
and feel so lost and empty
you got "no other choice" but to leave...
the existential allegory to never fully grieving
(for yourself) thus eternally feeling guilty and angry
always feeling the need towards running and escaping
 jean-paul sartre's existential state of "nausea" of being
and non-being the protoplasmic state of dreaming which
is simply the desolate inevitable truths and non-truths of reality
which is irrelevant or inconsequential whether it is happening
or not happening to know that dreaming is the ultimate hyperbole
to the great nihilistic philosophical decree of *i think therefore i am*
and so your ship hits the sand reef and you go off to start exploring

64. *To-Do List*

1. horse gets long lashes squeegied at gas station
2. roosters lined up for haircuts
3. ships put back in wilderness
4. rafts dragged to dockhouse
5. excavators build cities around pornographic strangers
    sprawled out on blind dates on romantic picnics
6. bones are discovered of the peeping tom & hypnotherapist

7. cats return home along with the comedians & convicts
8. a ribbon-cutting ceremony for the new mental health clinic with the mayor & child molester's mother & madmen & monster running the whole gig with his manufactured grin & when snapshots taken they all take their place in the pyramid
9. zarathustra and bodhisattva meet up at the bottom
10. it is apparent their dreams have gotten the better of them

65. *Grocery List*

reads milk
& medicine

reach out for sunbeam bread
coffin avenue, new bedford...

1. secretary with eternal hiccups
2. contemplating traffic going in
   and out of providence at dusk
3. "no, we don't have a dr. schwartz"
4. white girl who bumps beautiful buttercup breasts
   up against a black woman's bare black belly
5. blue boy beyond belief
6. how our doctor believed that even
   in bellies babies develop personalities
7. how our godmother tried to commit suicide recently
8. how everything started in the bronx and ended in brooklyn
9. and in the middle a queen and midtown manhattan
10. the image of a civil war wife ironing her husband's uniform
11. leaving a love letter in lunch box
12. junkies and drunkards skimming rocks
13. convinced dog is dressing up like drag queen sneaking out the
    house to blow hasidim and "world's greatest pop," whistling–
    she's a brick houuuse!
14. midnight orchids sprinkled in dew in the heather gardens
    of cloisters with wild winds coming in off the hudson
15. how she got fresh with you in the shadows
16. fiancées looking forward to the future

17. with wonderful sounds of faraway engines and sirens
18. never quite sure if cats were yowling or baby crying
19. g.i. joe being casually flung out a tenement window
    by a puerto rican boy parachuting down to safety
20. to thimbles filled with rain
21. naked dolls in the alley
22. old latino men lazily playing dominoes
    all night on midnight summer corners
23. over old boxes of sweet plantain
24. with widow wives praying
25. in winter they'll drag radio flyers
    with cases of beer through blizzards
26. past saintly daughters and old sicilians
27. past barbers and brownstones and cathedrals
28. and brilliant derricks on the river
29. how punchlines always seem like cruel lies at the expense of others
30. how to avoid bad dreams fall asleep to smell of orange rinds
    and cold red wine on ice

66. *Axe Of Kindness*

and so you set up guest dosing
for december 25th and december 26th
day and day after christmas so if by chance
you might hear one of your kids complaining
about some robot or contraption or thing he didn't
get just think of that chick whose husband used to cheat
and beat the shit out of her and now lives in a halfway
house out in new bedford and is simply grateful to do a 2
day visit with her mother and father on the outskirts of boston
and get her guest dose on the 25th and 26th of december over
at c.s.a.c. better known as "community substance abuse center"

67. *Somewhere Between Racing Thoughts And Reality*

and when you have them sit down to do
empty chair therapy it is most interesting
to see how the females start to express their
true emotionality and begin emoting as evidenced
in how poorly old boyfriends used to treat them

and in no longer having the ability to trust
or even know how to act when they find
someone who really cares for them and
with the male species little things
such as having no gas left

in their tank to even get home
as though they have subliminally
sentimentally let down some symbolic
loved one eternal mother or father figure

or even worst of all their selves
and will bury head in hand
and start to sob—

"i am such a fuckup!"

how much
we have to learn
from these lost souls

68. *Lo* & *Behold*

take for example how this keen client of mine
told me how she could always spot a cop
by his shoes and haircut and wristwatch

as all i could really do was sit back and smile and nod
feeling intrigued to be talking to her knowing how
others perceive and misconceive with pre-

conceived notions these "patients" as simply being
a bunch of madmen and hustlers and me knowing
them to be so much more perceptive and elevated

their only crime
that they just
wanted

to get out of
the cold and
feel warm all over

(and they're the first
ones to admit it self-
effacing and humble)

she told me later on that she was in the midst
of reading mark twain's what do you call that novel about the
leaping bullfrog while at the same time the original wizard of oz

she also told me how people
had always thought her stupid
and if they only knew how lucid

the head nurse steps out of the pill room
and gives a great big sigh at the end of her shift
then lumbers down the long white hall like the rest

of us stiffs like some rundown
wind-up doll with aching
ancient bones

69. *And You Close With*

asking him what he plans to do this weekend
and getting an instant quick straight answer–

"i'm gonna play
trouble with my girl"

upon further probing he cleverly comically
without even knowing fleshes out answer–

"she likes to play trouble"
she's twenty-four years old

70. *How It Goes*

knowing without a doubt how some old fisherman, exotic dancer,
ex-convict, abused woman, can put it all in perspective
with only one simple expression, simple catch phrases–

 "they got me on a buck 35"
 "how ya doing?"
 "high as a kite"

71. *How It Grows*

and you finally slip out your bleak office
into the blessed light of some indian summer
to experience and witness the salty lick of fresh
fish and red brick which transcendently splits
through all sadness and madness of ancient
existence and postmodern bullshit of all suffering
and loss and can see why someone might suddenly
decide to give it all up and go with instincts or what
we in our profession like to call poor impulses addict-
ive personality and stick a needle in flesh in a last
ditch effort to try and spiritually forgive and forget

72. *How It Glows*

and you head back home
through all those old
charcoal cathedrals

lego-like chimneys
strange and sad cities
in a valley of industry
back up the highway
down to the bones of
the sea where no one
could possibly find me
only maybe except me

73. *Structures Of Frank Lloyd Wright*

people don't
really know me

o well–
the coffee

maker reads
midnight

74. *Love Letter To Wife*

"was worried
about you
in the wind"

75. *And So Be It*

i want to hate
to find a way to die

to
dream...

getting lost in the murky shadows
of historic towns old ghost cities

of the east has always
been my mental hell

snow in window sill
and moon in the hills

nobody knows
the troubles

(always found male bonding so
corny, lonely, obvious, obscene

their *punch-lies* made
up of petty insecurities

you want to talk about
women gossiping?)

once wrote an aphorism—
"just past self-destruction's heaven"

like crumbling mansions
on a tumultuous sea

junkie no different
than the breeze

through
bending tree

than you
or me...

Part II:

The Life & Times Of The Man Sawed In Half

For The Kids

"I'm like a bird, I only fly away...
I don't know where my home is
I don't know where my soul is"

-Nelly Furtado

4 a.m.

wandering dark home
naked alone bare boned
nightmare after nightmare
after nightmare after nightmare
you suddenly look back and know
and understand your childhood
why you were so damn self-
destructive and accident-
prone and didn't know
probably wanted
to just let go
to give up
to sacrifice self
to kill yourself
on a daily basis
wild child
you
were
so
out of
control
desperately
trying to gain
some form of control
and go to the refrigerator
to drink cold milk to hope
to heal soothe and coat
your beaten and
battered soul
the lights of
the paperboy
come into
the dead
end like
a film
noire
and it
is only
the deep

and rickety
rhythmic
breathing
of cicadas
which gets
you back home

5:00

acorns have started to fall
from the great big oak which
hangs outside your window like
some brilliant ominous umbrella
adorned with these gems of fall as
all you hear is the echoing thud onto
the hood of your car outside your home

5:15

and think the only
thing you can rely on
the only thing reliable
are the garage doors
which go up just at
the right time every
time across the road
and babysitter who comes
out like some female super
hero with her perfect little
neat and tidy organized
steps and think i want
to follow them back
to where it all
went wrong

then forward
to try and make
sense of it all...

5:30

unable to sleep
i want to spoon
my wife 'neath
the stars till
the end of
eternity

5:45

black velvet top hats
of jet-black crows perched
like puppets up on top tippy-toes
way a top ancient fuzzy lichen fir trees

who keep an eye out on me
who keep me from feeling excruciatingly lonely
who keep me from doing something fucked-up and crazy

6:00

before you leave home
you put a little sticky
on the fish bowl

telling her
you love her

6:15

somewhere in florida, california
chameleons make their way in

6:30

when the sun comes up
you notice some flashing neon figure
of paul revere on his clattering horse

gracefully galloping
off over the colorful
dappled trees of autumn

in minuteman origami hat
perched, eager, reading
just below—"don't litter"

sun rising over methadone
clinic of moby dick marina
golden arches of mcdonalds

and beautiful black girl
in silhouette shuffling to school
over the iridescent catwalk of rush hour

7:00

driving into work leaving
with the exact same primal scream
as upon returning like one of those

man-made mourning and
mysterious howling persian
haunted holy pilgrim mecca cities

7:10

all the corn
which has grown
like mansions over
the gas station has been
taken out of the ground

and all that's left
are the brilliant copper
golden bamboo stalks like
some great glowing shroud
from a post-apocalyptic town

7:15

dusty children's faces pasted against windows
are whisked in school buses around dead
ends to lost vague amorphous destinations

they will get such reports back as—
"very nice kid but refuses to take off jacket
always feels the need to be the class clown

has such potential, needs to be tested
walks around the hall like he's got the
weight of the world on his shoulders "

7:30

this morning while driving into work
out to the mental health clinic
right around plymouth
i heard myself
chanting *rage against the machine*
dedicated purely to abuse of power
breaking of confidence supervisor—

"fuck you i won't do what you tell me!
fuck you i won't do what you tell me!
fuck you i won't do what you tell me!
fuck you i won't do what you tell me!"
a modern day bartleby the scrivener
passing the *pilgrim sand's motel*
literally right where the pilgrim's
stepped off and landed thinking
of that teenager from way back
in the day from that great comedy
"fast times at ridgemont high"
who simply got fed up
delivering fast food
in his hi-ho matey
pirate uniform
and tears it all off
pirate hat and all
and chucks the
whole damn thing
out the window
and think how i'd
like to simply follow
that star-spangled
sun kissed corvette
wherever it goes
zooming off
all the way
to the end
of the world
somewhere
anywhere
maybe even
provincetown
or p-town
think that's
what it's called
but don't know
maybe i'll just
save up and settle
for a chinese meal

to try and make
sense of it all

7:45

inspector clouseau still in all his disguises
his moustache & beard & bifocals
drives his little white paint truck
through the village, suspicious

sincere & earnest
destined & determined
humming his harmless hymns
to keep himself centered, grounded

8:00

*

i know the fall is here by the density
strength and length of the opaque
clouds laying low in the morning

*

lagoon getting dimmer
and trees brighter

*

last dewy blast
of perennial gardens

*

when i see all these assholes tailing each other
i start to think about the concept of heaven
if it's all just attention-seeking behavior?
who you know? nepotism?

can't even fathom
and if they're admitted
pretty sure i absolutely
don't want any part of it

*

instead of saying a prayer to myself
i hear myself muttering mantras
mumbling just to get by

*

the sign for martha's vineyard ferry
ripped off and it just reads—

"eyard ferry" and like
that so much more

*

income tax & tea
thai bangkok cuisine

milk
lottery

angels
oils

roses
shiners
worms

welcome
pilgrims

bus reads—
mayflower link

*

you imagine the back of an oil truck reads
"shipwrecked" and the last of the empty

flatbed dropping off remains
of carnival freak show set

*

they put the old timers
out in the cranberry bogs again

men in raincoats
in a field of pumpkins

Noon...

and get lost at last at the *whitehorse general store*
right next door to the post office and graveyard
with a dim light always on behind woebegone

ghostly time-stained curtains of lopsided
ramshackle rockinghorse shelters

on a seesaw ocean
of splintered stilts
and stray dogs

and shotgun seagulls
with soar throats wailing
soliloquies for the ages

bathed in opaque magnifying glass light
of some haunted season when the tourists
finally leave and natives gradually creep back in

young dirty down to earth
beat blue collar workers
already returning home
with booze and spirits

during dwindling days to fix
stranded shipwrecked souls

a cure to all those good
ol cold weather-worn
new england floors

in the splish-splash somersaulting shore
you call up your wife to tell her–
"i loved your supper
last night, thank you!"

12:15

then hear yourself casually saying aloud—
"can you make a list to take out the lint?"
and even start to think is this what it all
comes down to, to this? then think just
a bit further and deeper and would love
to take out all the lint, all that built up
bullshit of all those past experiences
which never got healed or fixed
anger and sadness which still
sits stirs sticks right between
the stomach and esophagus
more specifically spoken
that place where we store
and keep it all in where we
always feel like we want to
just explode want to break
down and cry for no particular
reason restless and agitated
and can't make sense of
it but just keep it all in
all that sadness and anger
more specifically spoken
and broken down and
sworn and articulated
which seems originally
like some idiot statement
but now that i stop to think
about it and dig a bit deeper
a pretty profound and trans-
cendent comment—
"can you make a list
to take out the lint?"

12:30

and it is only until later
until much later on

that you realize
everything *is*
pavlov's dog
certain women
girls seasons
moments
transitions
cops
crab
apples
bagels
and lox
all realized
in revelations
at the drive-thru
during a rain storm
and even more so not so
much even these images and forms
but everything that came before
the cause and core the cause
to exactly what and where
and why and who you are

12:45

at lunch break sitting at the end of world
where they came in from the old world
searching for the new world and think

i really want to go back to some
form of old world way before any
of this folklore ever existed before

there is a broken window in a dim home
which looks out to the choppy ocean
to the sails and ghosts and seasons

where all the transcendent dreams
and nightmares and fantasies
and visions seep in

exact same seagull
simple skull and all
on skipping stone shore

who stands there
pensive reflecting
tender thoughtful

and wonder what it was like
when they first came around
spotless bend and spotted land

and declared land-ho!
which turned to holy cow!
to holy cannoli! to hidi-hidi-hidi-ho!

back to group home
boys and girls on the run
through thick pine and pachysandra

1:15

now all it is *is* perfect pachysandra
shrubs and hedges, dewy fences,
steeples, candles, pipes & ladders,
cops in drizzle, pretty jogging wives
and mothers, bed and breakfasts

1:30

you wonder when the stooges
are gonna show up with their
big blocks of ice and pianos

2:30

kids gone forgotten and unnoticed
enraged cause they literally really
are forced to fight the system

enraged from the original abuse
and neglect that put them in
enraged from all those

anachronism which
could give a headache
to a god damn aspirin!

enraged cause of all the bozo idiot
clowns gathered around the clinical table
offering them old clichéd hand-me-down advice

simply following some agenda and protocol
and don't know their ass from their elbow
don't have the experience

don't know the half
or even an inch

so decide just simply to go
it on their own, on the run
maybe for just one single
moment, day, even month

in one last mad
dash for freedom

last but not least seen
on the side of the road

looking for someone
some home they never had before
whisked from group home to foster home
from literal wicked step mom to aunts to uncles

so young
with spirit
and soul

the children & crows
& cat-calls & cathedrals
incarceration & resurrection
crushed dandelion & dappled specimens

2:45

beautiful tomboy
dogged us all
in basketball

(and let us all
know about it
leaving even

the toughest of boys
talking to themselves
muted heads hung low)

think they all
fell in love
with her

3:00

turkey vultures
come up to visit
from deep woods

then recede
just as natural
into brush of trees

like some old
acquaintance you didn't
even know you were missing

3:30

just started this job
and can already see
through the snobs & slobs

already—
"i'd prefer not..."
"i'd prefer not..."

already humming good old dylan—
"it's just people's games
that you got to dodge..."

already bullshit
already bloodshot
already brainwash

4:00

i literally find myself leaning back in clinical
chair gargling iced coffee aloud thinking
how i'm gonna spend my paycheck
later on tonight and surprise the wife
hope she likes what i'm gonna get
her for the playroom and not be
angered or disappointed with
my impulse control disorder

4:35

looking out from my porthole
at the bottom of the ship
at the end of my shift

(where you see seasons shift
from deep beneath trees
of basement)

i hear my colleague's radio—
"boogie nights are always
the best in town..."

5:00

taking off to the smell of cinnamon
popovers and pork chops and *the enterprise*
newspaper still wrapped up in a bundle on the porch

Sundown...

*

you want to grab
your wife's hand

till the end of time
whichever one

lets go
first

*

they're putting
back together

the sagimore bridge balanced below
glowing flow of twilight gorilla moon

5:15

to get a little
feel and flavor
of the real world
of culture whatever
you want to call it
you always take
the long way
and blissfully
stray back home
through a very
strange repressed
eccentric town
of beautiful clowns
jesus fanatics
and dope addicts
firemen decked out
in their proud
buckle up
button down
firemen outfits
black and white bums
leftover gigolos by
the movie theater
judges with drinking
problems goth boys
and runaways
windy witches
wild-bearded
suspender-wearing

whitman electricians
wino cowboy heroin
addicts in ten
gallons with
bowlegged
wooden
legs
shuffling
up from the river
beautiful young
pornographic
daughters
fragile fathers
good mothers
rich kids turned
to designer drugs
and self-destructive
behavior the joggers
monuments coming
to life on the corner
the paper-mâché
cathedrals and
tin foil steeples
state hospital
state forests
and just around
the bend plymouth
rock with graffiti
scribbled all over it
as you return home
exhausted bloodshot
through cranberry bogs
and placid magic wand
paint-by-number ponds
gigantic splintered spindles
of real rough and tough
lincoln log rubber cement
sawdust fairydust forests
sea captain homes
bread and butter
butterscotch

bone-colored
with their great big
whiskey wraparound
widow watch creaky
candle hush hush secrets
in the waning windows
the little alabaster
ice cream girls
of the swamp
and sun-
streaked sun
pulled back
through
blazing
blonde hair
with silly
lily-white
seductions
in jackie o.
sunglasses
way before
the trend
even started
good clean-cut
boys diligently
driving trucks
as young as
newly-cut wood
just stacked up
the studs picking
up their liquor
and firewood
mischievous
flamboyant
delinquent
cops & robbers
pilgrim indians
crawling
on hands
and knees
through the

transcendent
pine needle brush
with foreign accents
and developing addictions
old antique book shop
and booze shop
in the dim
off season
golf courses
and resorts
ice cream
stands just shut down
the drowsy boxcar diners
and splintered homes
down long sandy
lopsided roads
last of pastel-colored
rafts of twinkling twilight
tucked into the setting
sun and when
you think about
this perfect neat
and tidy little part
of town can't help
but to feel just
a little let down
a little down
and out
mild drab
flickering
brilliant sort of
somber reflection
heading homebound
past weird mcmansions
of gleaming faux pillars
alongside the highway
right past that little
piece of lake
where it always
smells exactly
like fried

calamari
corn bread
and angel
food cake
and know
right there
and then
you are
on your way
undercover cops
with nothing better
to do than pick on
pick up mexicans
in the dawn of dusk
in their sleeping bags
along the side
of the road
your down
in the dump
mug shot
redeemed reborn
laid to rest beneath
a beautiful blotted
long gone sun

Dusk...

it all smells like one of those
big old custard boston cream donuts
when the sun falls down and sky breaks opens
and the light like the aperture to one of those

brilliant 24 hour all-night diners lost and alone
and laid out in orange blaze sugar maples
horizon like a great big sloppy
cheeseburger with raw onions

pretty young girl holds open windy door...

5:45

that great big half wolf half dog
on his last leg still wandering
staggering tip-toeing proudly
sniffing exploring the dead end
and dappled leaves of autumn

just a bit slower a bit sadder
more pensive more reflective
a little deaf a little blinder
yet still so much
more alive

so much more
sacred caring
compassionate
kinder than any of these
so called upstanding citizens

6:00

you think you want to disconnect the dots. of these connect
the dot people. who live in their connect the dot worlds.
with their convenient disconnects. and try to connect
yours. convenient and comfortable. ignorant and arrogant.
insular and delusional. phony to the bone. and play roles
without soul. know-it-alls who don't know a thing at all.

and pass judgment and passive-aggressive behavior
without an ounce of experience. integrity or honor.
nor what they're most guilty of. don't know a thing
about you. your heart and soul. kindness and com-
passion. your gut and generosity. everything you been
through. the sacrifices and the suffering and struggle.

and seen it all...

you think back to all those good ol episodes who
was that? the stooges? chan? chaplin? little rascals?
abbot and costello? really doesn't much matter anyhow
where there was one of those man-made knotholes dug
into ol black & white static depression industrial residential
picket fences and how these classic hysterical slapstick
thieves and delinquents sticking curious and mischievous
sockets through it would graciously let you in and find out
everything that's really happening and very much feel that
that's the true core reality experience if you ever really cared
to look at it from the real righteous point-of-view and perspective

6:15

you think that any one of these kids
that you work with out at the
group home in plymouth
massachusetts

have far deeper and kinder and more creative souls
than any of these devils who own homes out here
on the dead end and try to pull you into their hole
simply all about control and playing their obvious

and predictable unconvincing roles
to engage you in petty and pathetic
trivial grown-up battles and wars.
he sits on top of the picnic table

after having been punched in the face
one too many times by his stepfather
and strums on his guitar the plaintive pink floyd solo—
  "so...so you think you can tell...heaven from hell..."

6:30

you think you
want to nod out
on dope while
being whipped
around in the
tea cups in
the magic
kingdom

then haul me off
with one of those
humongous hooks

while still
nodding
out in
my mickey
mouse ears—

"book your own
special disney
vacation down
in orlando
florida"

6:45

fallen decorative pear
holds up the skull
of scarecrow
slouching in
lawn chair

as a kid couldn't keep yourself
out of trouble just like these kids
but always knew how quick and
clever and smart you really were

7:00

drizzle falls
on the dwarf
watermelons

at dusk
on the table
on side of the road

7:30

the shadows of the dragonfly
and hummingbird buzz past
the last blast of geraniums

can't tell you how much i miss
the aroma of formaldehyde streaming
from the windows of *south brooklyn casket*

along with the hanging puerto rican
sisters hollering their dreams
wishes and illuminations

when the last of the fall sun falls
on cobblestone creating pools
of deep splashing shadows

7:45

so now we look from our suicidal homes
at the change of seasons feeling out here
eternally stranded and know we are long
gone when we're not sure which one is
going into which one not really sure if
any that matters get to know neighbors

by their dogs by their daughters by
good girls who are babysitters and
take care of our children and knew
them when they were so young
now somehow waving at them
in the front seat of their cars.

when those alien robots
finally do show up it will
be right at the bottom of
the above-ground pools

ore-ida french
fry salesman
who once went
to culinary school
returns back home
when the day is done

hoping to squeeze out
just a little more sun
so he may make his
grand escape on his
bat boat to the horizon

tree frogs go on...

8:00

homes stand out here
like museums and mausoleums
and man don't see a single soul out
here but the gardener and the mailman

garage doors
magically going up
then going down again

martian light on in the window
the neighbor on his tractor with
his light beer and lights on then
vanishes like a ghost into thin air

8:15

take to the top of my stairs
and just sitting there up on top
(like a pot of gold at the end of
the rainbow) is a little jar of *vicks vapo
rub* and one of those droppers for the nose

always know there's a certain
part of the stairs a certain
part of the home where
the meals the stews
the casseroles flow

autumnal vegetables
the sweet squash
the eggplant
the turnip
native corn

the crows go in
and drizzle falls
on the hibiscus
in the midst of
misty foyer

8:30

on kitchen island reads
a note from kid's teacher—

"thank you for the
paper dolls & popcorn"

8:45

ladybugs creeping all over
the pastel-colored walls
of pink and pale-green
and blush and coral

buddha heads
resting their bones
on the coffee table
with son in bathtub

pointing his index finger
giving you permission
to dream of unicorns
and rainbows

9:30

dog is let down
scuttles down
down into
deep dark
basement
where just
the sacred
beacon from
tom & jerry
flashes all the day long
and will fall asleep down
there on the quilted rockers

10:00

all the haystacks
all the mums
all the white
and orange
pumpkins
have been
set and displayed
in front of the home
all the tulip bulbs below
all the acorns and pine cones
and pine needles have fallen
all the suns and moons
all widows and winos
all the leaves
and crab apples
and fall fast asleep
and sink into your
easy chair
right in front
of the great
red river rivalry
getting ready
for dreams
for nightmares
for a new day
of sleepwalking

Midnight:

it is true it is really only cumming
feeling like you're going crazy
breaking down crying being
born dying dreaming that
are your one and only
instincts your fish
from satiny siam
every evening

keeping you
company
drinking
your wine
minding
his own business
me minding mine

what happened to those good
old chinese joints where
they used to give you
those warm and wet
wash cloths you'd
throw over your
head to hope
to heal all
the lies?

the stolen piece
of apple pie
and wine

Sunrise: morning tide

at dawn you sleep like jesus the night before
it all happens in your dreamworld
your girl gets up and tells you–

it was all so real
then it was gone.

About the Author

Joseph Reich is a social worker who works out in the state of Massachusetts; a displaced New Yorker who sincerely does miss dissplace, most of all the Thai food, Shanghai Joe's in Chinatown, the fresh smoothies on Houston Street, and bagels and bialy's of The Lower East Side. He has a wife and handsome little boy with a nice mop of dirty-blonde hair, and when they all get a bit older, hopes to take them back to play, to pray, and contemplate in the parks and playgrounds of New York City.

He has been published in a wide variety of eclectic literary journals both here and abroad and his most recent books include, *A Different Sort Of Distance* (Skive Magazine Press), *If I Told You To Jump Off The Brooklyn Bridge* (Flutter Press), *The Derivation Of Cowboys & Indians* (Poet Works Press), *Obscure Aphorisms Written On A Fine Overcast Day* (Lummox Press), *Escaping Shangrila* (Punkin House Press), *Drugstore Sushi* (Thunderclap Press), *Bally's: A Didactic Case Study On The Human Species* (Alternating Current Co-op), and *The Path Of The Crow* (Alternating Current Co-op).

.

www.ingramcontent.com/pod-product-compliance
Lightning Source LLC
Chambersburg PA
CBHW052135090426
42741CB00009B/2083